The Shared World

POEMS

Vievee Francis

TriQuarterly Books / Northwestern University Press
Evanston, Illinois

TriQuarterly Books
Northwestern University Press
www.nupress.northwestern.edu

Printed in the United States of America

10 9 8 7 6 5 4 3 2 1

Library of Congress Cataloging-in-Publication Data

Names: Francis, Vievee, author.
Title: The shared world : poems / Vievee Francis.
Description: Evanston : TriQuarterly Books/Northwestern University Press, 2023.
Identifiers: LCCN 2022032709 | ISBN 9780810145191 (cloth) |
    ISBN 9780810145214 (ebook)
Classification: LCC PS3606.R3653 S53 2023 | DDC 811/.6— dc23/
    eng/20220804
LC record available at https://lccn.loc.gov/2022032709

To Matthew Olzmann

And I looked around that gate of late and weary ones and I thought, This is the world I want to live in. The shared world.

—Naomi Shihab Nye

CONTENTS

III

IV

V

The Shared World

TO FORGET

Ô douleur! ô douleur! Le Temps mange la vie,
Et l'obscur Ennemi qui nous ronge le cœur . . .
—Charles Baudelaire, "L'ennemi"

Welcome the enemy back with flags of forgetfulness.
Let the children go forward yelping as innocents so often do.
Make a line, stand in the old formation. Believe! Believe!
The cells are empty, flesh gone, bones buried,
unrecognizable. How well the enemy looks, no
longer gaunt. So plump, as if something young were had
for breakfast. Look! A pick in the tooth. Hooray!
Bring the enemy back at night by boat or plane.
Allow the enemy the crossing. Let them
make a grand entrance on the square in the light
of the morning. In clean white clothes and a handkerchief
at the side of the mouth. Let us forgive as the Books would
have us do. So what the dead past. Only the old dare
remember and they are without teeth. So be it, the gone,

                                              gone—

Hasn't the enemy been through enough?
Wasn't the enemy there?

came as the lanterns floated upward
on a night of celebration and as flares spun upward out of the fear
of those who set them, as shawled women smiled in the night,
prayed into the night, and just as many ran through the swallowing
night, as a bed was shared between those shepherding each other
and as others shared nothing, nothing at all, as doctors took their oaths
and committed no harm, privileging some, denying others, as another
dies by the hands of a group of strangers, and another by the hand
of her father, and another because a stranger was lost in the anger
of his mother.
                              I am telling you the call to arms came
as we slept and as we marched, as we questioned and as we hid
our heads in the dust of nostalgia or our spent dreams, as bills came due,
as the debt grew and values diminished, as women decided other women
            mattered less,
as we raged and as we ignored and the doors began to close and close and close
and close and close and those who had opened them were marked for death
or forgetting, and those who kick them down are marked for death or slander,
and this is not the first time a call to arms has caught us imagining it had stopped,
the call is ever, is constant, don't you hear it? Don't you? What? It didn't ring
out in a peal of bells? It rings out in the silent appeals of children, a child
who cannot remember the name of their father. You aren't listening. And
if you are listening, you must keep your ear to the street, to the field, to
the alleys and bridges, to the riverbed and floor planks of abandoned houses,
and I heard the call to arms like a moan from a drain, desperately clogged, and
in the lowing of cows in drought, in the impotent drone of senators, that officious
blather, and in this moment I hear the call and realize I am not the lion but
the antelope and I must resort to my feet and my wits amid a storm of teeth and
            claws
on a day that began as any other day, and I can't tell you why I hear
what too many refuse to admit, like the pounding of your own heart
            upon hearing this.

BREAK ME AND I'LL SING

My voice like marrow, a blood-yolk
spilled upon the counter. You can't stop this
song. More hands than yours have closed
around my throat. You may crack me.
You have cracked me. I'm frightened
but so what? I'll testify. Witness,
if you can, listen: I slurped the frog-leg soup
gone bad. Held a brass spoon like a barrel
to my mouth. I could tell you what you want
to hear, but I'd be broken just the same,
                              so why not sing?
I'm singing now, louder this time and in the round:
We are a-wounding of red-plumed birds. Every voice,
a bloody feather in the bone crown.

I

The doll was a smaller version of myself
though I had never been there before: heavy-
ankled, with braided hair (even the part down the middle),
breasts that speak of all that is equatorial and
nothing at all of the northern climes. The face
was not outwardly sloped (as mine is not). The brow
was a medium brow, neither protuberant
nor hairless (as in removed, as is the fashion in some
places). The neck and shoulders of the doll were
closer than would be considered desirable in the West
but I wasn't in the West. Nothing was quick. Nothing
convenient. Nothing smelled of strawberries or
the ubiquitous cherry. Pinkless, the doll was darker
than me (myself) made of ebony (?) or some such wood.
It was all of a piece. Its feet were heavy, as if the carver
had not taken time with them. No time is taken
with mine. The rounded underbelly being lifted
so the beads around the waist could be presented.
One strand to represent many. Though
there were differences. The scarring. On the doll,
intentional and vertical. On me, horizontal
and not beautiful in the eye of any beholder
but a doctor admiring his handiwork, his way
with scalpel and stitch. Still, we both showed
the evidence of our age. I held her as if
I were a little girl. She had the face of a woman.
She was hard but could be broken. I am
only as hard as I need to be and have been
broken many times. No one seemed to find it odd
there in the market. The obvious American
holding tightly the Ghanaian doll, rocking it
back and forth in the bassinet of her arms,
cooing, *It's OK. It's OK. It will all be OK.*

ANOTHER ATTEMPT AT THE TELLING

*The secret story is the one we'll never know, although
we're living it from day to day . . .*
　　　　　　　　　　　　　　　　—Roberto Bolaño

But—
we do know *the secret story*. At least, we each know our own secret
story, and when we grow brave enough might share it,
and if the party we share it with is honest, they might admit
their own, and from there, hands held, we walk into the grotto
and dip our hands into the cold waters, or meander up
a darkened stairwell into the sweet musk of a bookshop, or
descend into a speakeasy beyond a roped velvet curtain.
The secret to knowing the secret is to speak, but we too often tell
the stories of no matter and avoid the one story that does matter.
In truth, we are bound by one story, so you'd think by now
we'd tell it, at least to each other.

1965

In Selma that day. The photograph. The way she is looking at him. Not his name. His pallor. Not the city nor the event, not even the blood on his neck. When I saw the picture I realized someone cared enough to take it. There was only one lens. Then, the entire world wasn't always watching. She pressed that cloth to his neck as intimately as a kiss whispered into the channel of an ear. Spontaneously. Sudden and overwhelming as a father's embrace after a father's failure to embrace. I was two years old. It was before I knew what I was born into. It would have been illegal for me to have married my husband. My husband stares at the picture and, enraged, considers the context and stakes. But a man so compassionate cannot easily take in its lack. It takes the violating or the violated to know. The reward of courage is this: My husband told his parents he would marry me. Period. He expected his parents to live up to the values they espoused. They have. If I cry, my blue-eyed father-in-law—whose own father left Germany during the nascent rise of Hitler—cries. Galway's eye to Harriet's, brown as mine. Look at the way he looks at her. Like a sun rising twice to be Galway that day looking into the face of the tender after terror. See, the grace of gratitude. He being there. She being her.

*

Years later, a movie about that day in Selma pressed time into a black box. A friend—who was the same age—gripped my hand. I imagined I knew him *then*, saw us as children together. Wondered if he would have wiped the blood from my mouth. He thought my tears were for those on the screen, but I cried too for my child self, the loneliness from a playground that has never left me. Harriet did not leave Galway. Finding him hurt after the billy club struck purchase made her even more herself. My husband always knows where to find me. A husband too young to have seen the signs but has learned them, says, *I wish you knew people like Harriet when you were little. I wish I had been there.* So he doesn't mind the care a friend shows me now. We held hands in a dark place, and it was a brief balm. Enough to keep me from fainting. And my husband draws me home, like a sandbox friend waiting for you after you've been punished for something you didn't do.

Into the bow of your ear I whispered the secret story. Now you can't sleep
    either.
                Consider it part of your own memory connecting our
                childhoods that would have
otherwise never crossed—I fell down and your knee was scraped; I stuffed
    the yellow cake into
            my mouth and your stomach cramped; when you were
            abandoned grief filled
my well—the private ravages of our spent youth, and adulthood now
    implicitly intimate.
                            You pull me to you because I
                          have already softened
              your sharp elbows.
The pressure of your fingers in my shoulder leaves
            an impression as if in need I had touched myself. We are
            insomniacs. The grip
of night freeing us from the slept-through day and its demands. It *is* true,
    once you know, you
            can't unknow, so we ruminate on literature and the gods
            and continually seek
        the ousia of the emptied jug. But we need no wine really. We are
        eager to get on with it.
To take in or do whatever forwards the living, this tripwire keeping us tied
                    kite to string, present to past, arrow
                to quiver.

HONEY

Every spring there was always a boy or two who dared
to press himself into the bees. In the mid-South
the free hives hang close to the bark
from limb to ground, taller than the tall boys
who would walk toward the mass
                    slowly
                        quietly—one arm held out
                            and a hand extended delicately
                                as a cotton fan into
                                    that susurration.
On a small college campus full of the brilliant,
the mundane, and the mad, boys, inevitably slender but sometimes
thinly muscled, would let the bees cover their shirtless bodies,
                        their hair and delicious skin.
                The loners, the eccentric, boys
                (always boys but why?)
                with their own voices sounding
                in their heads. But
                                I'd like to think
                it was music they heard, the song of bees,
                        their dislocated thrum most know to dread.
I would watch from the distance
and admire their willingness to inhabit what others didn't
dare consider.
                A few years ago, miles from any home
I'd known, I walked along an avenue where great bundles
of flowers hung just overhead   I stopped.
                        There were just a few bees
                                but enough.

I have been allergic to them all my life. Always carrying an antidote.
Always afraid. But I wanted to know what I had to lose. So,
            into those blooms, I thrust my arms
                      up to the elbows—
No bees stung me, but I fell breathless on the grass and
thought of those boys, so beautifully drawn.
                                Such reckless hosts.

Every time I open my mouth my teeth reveal
more than I mean to. I can't stop tonguing them, my teeth.
Almost giddy to know they're still there (my mother lost hers)
but I am embarrassed nonetheless that even they aren't
pretty. Still, I did once like my voice, the way it moved
through the gap in my teeth like birdsong in the morning,
like the slow swirl of a creek at dusk. Just yesterday
a woman closed her eyes as I read aloud and
said she wanted to sleep in the sound of it, my voice.
I can still sing some. Early cancer didn't stop the compulsion
to sing but there's gravel now.
An undercurrent
            that reveals me. Time and disaster. A landslide
down the mountain. When you stopped speaking to me
what you really wanted was me to stop speaking to you. To
stifle the sound of my voice. I know.
Didn't want the quicksilver of it in your ear.
                  What does it mean
to silence another? It means I ruminate on the hit
of rain against the tin roof of childhood, how I could listen
all day until the water rusted its way in. And there I was
putting a pan over here and a pot over there to catch it.

ON THE PINEY WOODS, DEATH, BOBBY FRANK CHERRY, AND ME

They move through the exit. The drama of their
earthly life comes to a close . . . These children,
unoffending, innocent, and beautiful.
> —Martin Luther King Jr., eulogy for the four girls
> killed in the Birmingham bombing, 1963

"He said he lit the fuse."
> —Testimony of Willadean Brogdon,
> ex-wife of Bobby Frank Cherry

Sometimes I wander around wondering
where my mother is. The family buried
her next to her own mother. Out there,
the hard pines darken early. Anyone
can hide and not be found for years.
Frank Cherry laid low there. The girls came
in his dreams. You can't live in those woods
and not be haunted by what you've done.
So he had to be more given to visitation
than most. They wouldn't have come whole;
they would have arrived in bits and pieces,
the way he left them. They would have held
bits of church brick and holy bric-a-brac.
One or two might have come as a glove or a hat
small enough for a child's head. I imagine
they were laughing or singing before the bomb
went off so they may have moved through
the house as voices or the tiny tap of a shoe.
I lived out there when he did. I didn't know
he was there. It makes sense. It was a place
inhabited by the lost and the found, by horror

and grace. I am haunted by memories as
present as ghosts. I believe in ghosts and am
grateful I have committed no crimes. Though
I am untouchable, I was born so. Under four
pounds, bent legged, pale and stricken. I
went straight into an incubator. A metal tit.
Monkeyed against a glass and metal frame.
The girls would have been only a few years older
than me. They died as I was born. They were blown
to the winds. I was born into the storm of them.
I cannot hold it all together. The pieces,
of them, of me. My mother hated my needing
to touch her. To have her in my sight. Young
and free enough to flit and flirt away into an evening.
I cried myself sick whenever she left. I wound
myself around her when she returned and
could feel the wince in her gaze, in her gloved
hands pushing me away. When we feel unloved,
does it matter who doesn't love us? She did not
hate me. No crime was committed. Had Cherry known
I lived down the road, he would have hated me.
l knew early on I could be blown to bits by any
white man with enough rage. Some are unwanted
and live. Some are erased. It is not a matter of degree.
It is a matter of intent. Those girls were loved.
Why aren't they here? Why am I?

swells the moon. And the eyes that look to it.
And your ears hear the keening move over and between
every living thing and through every dead one.
When stabbed, if stabbed more than once, a threshold is reached—
The point of no return.   A horizon
                    that holds no other   horizon—
the pain keeps. But the blood flows out   wending its way as saltwater
                                                        finds its level.
The sound of the wound like the sound of the wounds is
constant. It can be withstood because it is always there—
                                                the keening.
A wail carrying what no one dares say. The truth
of the matter. There is always a need.
Always hands empty. And love, love so fickle and feckless. An empty house
and dog at the door. Or a man clutching his sobs, willing to devour or deny
                    what he craves for those he does not.
See the crow at the tail of a vulture.
                    A vulture ever coveting something more majestic
than itself.
                    And there—a child eaten by its father. A child stewed by its mother,
punched into tenderness.   The bones bro-
ken, rebrok-en, then set madly in the splint.
                    A dirty girl is swallowed whole by a man dirtier still.
                    The flowers are always taken for trash, but
the trash is always ringed in gold.
                              A gloss of beauty dispossessing
                              beauty. A failing of the eye
                              and
a woman who mourns it all. The crier,
needled by a splinter in the cornea
                    and tears that connect us all.

are not writing poems for beauty's sake.
Their poems come in bottles from the sea
to be put to our ears like conches.
There are poems buried in the sands
of prison yards, backyards, sequestered
under stones, stone that was once the walls
of a city, of a station, of a house, of a room in the heart
of a house.
        Poems are torn from the hidden notebooks
of poets in hiding. Poems are disguised
as tails on long-stringed kites, are given to carrier
pigeons disguised as more common birds.
Some poems fall, or are thrown down. Wads
like grout between cracked tile.
        The poets who are ours
to battle may lose everything to pipes, to wire and glass,
to objects simple enough to be found in a cabinet.
These poets may die by fast talkers, by mistake, by gun, by bomb,
and some by God by choice. The poets write to us
of children and of strangers. They write
with fingers in their ears to hear themselves think.
Their poems are the only thing clear where little else is
clear. The poems speak of a meal of lemons, of baskets
in an alley, of leather, and of the sea. Always the sun-
swallowing sea.
        The poets who are our enemies are not writing
for a canon, their letters black as smoke
filling an emptied square. They are writing for their lives.
Some are dead already
by the time their poems finally reach us.
Their letters, bold as the cry of a dog heard over shells.
Poems that speak plainly of a hand that seeks
a hand but, finding nothing, reaches still.

nothing more than to be held by your brother
and within that absence to be held by
another. It will take that to cry it through.
And if there is no one to do so, if
there is an embrace but it does not last
long enough—
                    you may never feel the joy of wailing,
                    instead, you may hold that cry for years,
until no one knew you ever needed
to cry at all. Until you believe you are free
of tears, until one day standing at the sink,
the water running hot over your knuckles,
you double over,
                    and that long-held cry escapes
in a gasp. A memory of that other body in convulsion,
the sickbed or the street, the smell of death so close
you forget there are people with you in the room
and you almost let go,

                    before you are reminded
that day is done and there is work before you to do,
so you straighten up and continue to do whatever it was
                              you were doing,
close the valve of ache, and swallow whatever came up.

The dress my mother died in   no
          the dress I was wearing when
my mother died
                         and
I took pictures of myself   self?   no
of the dress   of my legs curled tight under
the dress   only my ankles and feet showing
I held my arm up and back
and
          did not want to show my head   my
     swollen eyes
and chapped lips   and all that dried salt
on my face
               my   face
she could not bear to look at   unless
it was with disgust   my hair
never good   no good   and my un-ironed
dress   this one   I am wearing now
with its white cotton underslip and its red
embroidered paisley upon a white background
It is   beautiful even
          with me in it   Yes   I am not
wearing a hat   She said, You look so ugly in that hat
It was my favorite one of three
          hats
She had more than one hundred hats stored in her
basement   in labeled hatboxes they
were her   particular thing   every Sunday a new
one   perched proudly as a bird-of-paradise
though only the males are so presentable
          but she was a tomboy once and
so was her mother   She hated my teacups

and my dollies that I couldn't sleep without
          like I slept that day when I found out
she had died   I lay fetal upon the bed
atop the duvet and wanted to live   and felt
guilt like a razor over the wrist   You always
were odd and always carrying on   You
talk too much   You are a mess   And I was
a mess   my chest wet and my heart
          shrinking in and I was
               shrinkingand this
               wasgood   She was
alwaysasmallwoman   except
                         for ten years
when she grew past what hersmallframe could hold
who can say why
          her hunger grew   and why
she hated my hungertobeheld and so   recoiled
and I went days and days without any touch at all
and I have gone days and days since   Ugly
in my hat   even my father thought so   though
now he isn't sure   Since she died so much
has changed   even this dress now
stained by wear and coffee and crying and   now the pills
won't let me
                         and now and again
sleeping in it   and just last night keeping it on for dinner
alone at the same counter where I was when
                         I found out she had died
a few minutes after our last phone call
                    when she couldn't see me and
                         so could afford to love me.

UGLY FRUIT

I just need to know you don't think I'm ugly, I said.
OK already, you're not ugly.

—Conversation between myself and a friend

Not knowing is worse, I said but didn't mean it.
It is just as bad knowing—
which means this ending. My abandon often
leads to abandonment, so I bury my face
in the bristling hawthorn. Did I tell you
everybody is beckoning to me? Even in loss
I can't help but admire the rough jaw, the knee
reddened from falling, a shoulder plump as
a dewy kumquat, and cheeks I would kiss and and and—
There was a woman whose mother had burned her
legs. The calves fire-licked. I still remember the touch
of them. I took off her shoes. I put my hands under
her thick socks. She cried at the feel of someone's hands.
When I am abandoned I wonder what I lack. I know
what I lack. My friends note:
                          I am "not ugly," sure,
like giving a bonus to the doorman, or an extra week's
vacation to the maid—you feel generous but the door keeps
being opened and shut, and the dishes get cleaned anyway.
There are scars that can't be seen.
                         I want them touched, but
there are more scars than hands willing. An acquaintance
fears her neighbor's amputated arms. A waiter gets bullied
for hair that doesn't fall upon his shoulders but moves out
and up mat from the head.   Call someone "ugly" for *any*
reason and my chest hurts, as if punched. I don't always see it
coming and I don't see the point because it is so often

all too fucking *beautiful* to me. All of you:

                                   the ravaged and the torn,

the denied and the haunting. Desire bristles in me

just the same. Does want get befuddled by cruelty? by abandonment

like bruised fruit in a bin. I can't always name them.

I pick them up anyway—a soup, a salad, unadorned in a spoon—

uneasy on the eye someone threw them out,

as if the eye must be always free of tears,

as if the eye was made to look away instead of toward.

is Detroit is Rome is Birmingham is Juárez is Accra is towns along the
Rio Grande, the congregations in Vermont is the Spree, the Detroit
River is Hanover, where the Connecticut River runs and my great-aunt's
ashes move with the silt. Is that professor. Is Fort Concho, then San
Angelo. Is a grandfather and his two wives. Snakes: the one my father
held up, the ones my brother kills with a sharp-edged spade. Provinces.
Provence. If one more person says they have a second home there. Why
tell me? Pistoia. The train with the lovely young man whom I would
have kissed on the way to Firenze. I see him in a husband. Oaxaca. The
Juárez of my father's memory. I asked a friend, Why stay in Berlin? No
one believes how hard it is to remain. How easily civilization slides into
conflagration. I don't hate most of my enemies. And the ones I do hate,
I want only to be free of. Bears at the screen door. Some think I am a
bear, but I am a rabbit. A fainting goat. A sheep my great love shepherds
away from the ledges. Did I say love? Love. We are obliged to. Ha! Ha! I
saw the young man in my father as I ran my fingers along the old stone
in Rome. Jefferson's slave should have stayed in Europe. But I've known
those who should have left. I want to walk the paths of my friends. With
my friends. I am a broken honey jar. One leg faltering. One half of me
denying the other. My friends are not interested. They bore easily. So I
walk up to and alongside strangers. There was a boy in Kumasi I wanted
to marry. I loved his first wife. We looked like sisters. I went back to
Detroit. Why? Friends give me the bible of themselves. Versions. I read
voraciously. I haven't smiled in seven generations. I ask an acquaintance,
Why stay in the South? Half is South. As much as half is West. When I
finally went forward to Africa, I collapsed and kissed the muddy tarmac
to the amusement of the Senegalese sipping Orange Crushes. But look at
me trying to tell you—
and I've tried before—I danced in Ghana. A moment that cannot be
repeated. So it is good I paid attention. Like the lips of the young man
on the train to Firenze that I imagined as soft in all of their fullness, like
mine. But I do not deny the delight of the mouth thinned into cynicism,
the mouth that never admits its own delight, because it is good to open,

26

even if only a little. The prickly pears have blossomed, their rumpled dark pinks more beautiful than any man's imaginings. Most things are. From Marfa I see a wall of mountains. Mexico on the other side. Or am I? But doesn't it all fall. Like history.

DEAD OR ALIVE, THE RATS IGNORE US

No one moves away—
as the rats, plump on refuse,
refuse to startle. Take the one by the sidewalk in front
of my neighbor's flat, its back humped
against the brick edging, hungrily
scraping, undulant and not bothering to turn
and face me walking up behind it—
choosing instead to stay and pack the holes
with steel wool or cement, or antacids (hoping
it's true that rats can't belch). I'm the one
who shouted, then looked around to see who heard
me so afraid. Too afraid to pass the creature
stuffing something wet and undefinable
under the masonry into its white-toothed mouth.
What we wouldn't give for just one good flautist.

JUNETEENTH (#3)

~~The blue wildflowers. The gulf a rare blue.~~
The gulf isn't blue, but see how pretty I want to make it
~~pretty~~. It was ugly then. How long it took. Dangerous.
~~That's it.~~ How ~~much was~~ many were kept ~~back.~~ for so long.
~~I should know.~~ I know. I am a descendant of those
who toiled in quiet ~~like me~~. And know how to keep my rage
behind my back ~~like a truck's load too wide for the lane.~~
I ~~understand~~ . . . I always ~~thought~~ believed it was more work
they wanted ~~from us,~~ those "masters of severance," ~~Lazy~~
bastards. ~~Now, I know they feared~~ Fearing what might be
loosed upon them. All the ragged horse tenders.
All the dust-bedraggled black skins, too proud to bow
and when they did, didn't mean it. I ought to know. I'm smiling
~~now~~, in your face because a freewoman bides her time.
Doesn't ~~readily~~ show ~~you~~ her hand . . .

THE SMELL

of death isn't always putrid. It may begin as the smell of roses.
          Something that expected and dull. Pale
tea roses under the windowsill of a mother who will turn toward you
and swing hard. Her small fist balled with the memory of someone else.
Or coffee, another common scent, like the sweat of sex, it opens the nose
to the morning. Recall a fresh burn on the skin, so like the cigarette stink
of a father who never wanted children but wanted everything else. Let's say
he dies in a bar, then death may be the stench of bourbon on bourbon
already spilled and stuck invisibly to the brown floor as a stain
that can't be seen. But, like horror, death can be foreseen, it can
reach the nose before the eyes. Horror is patient, may wait in some
dim room, a room from which wafts the smell of cabbage, or perhaps
dampness, mold. The perfume of a rumor. The smoke of a field
after bodies release their scent of release. Look for death
where there is the suggestion of rain in the air or a heavy whiff of smog.
Look everywhere. Pay attention to the winds, which way they blow, and
if toward you, don't be lulled into believing the air won't be sweet with snow.

ACCIDENTAL CITY

after Jacek Dehnel

From the distance the squares
                    within squares.
A few blocks of streets and alleys and
small parks and . . . closer . . .
windows open to vodka and
apple juice coating the bar counters,
a dim light penetrates the stained and thinning
curtains of storefronts to fall upon
gartered mannequins rusting on the tiles.
All the frayed edges.
I was a beggar holding out my cracked cup.
Thieves? No one stopped them.
Just a foot away—the road.
A few more feet—the tracks.
No one came to lift me from my solitude.
From the pitiless city of myself.
The maze buzzed. Everyone scurried along.
Once I decided to move on, the space I occupied
filled mercilessly behind me. A horde
of hapless skirts and hounds. A man
took over the curb. He wore a coat
of shredded newspaper. Couture of obits
and headlines. My mouth sank
into the glassy eye of my regrets. The sad light
said go. I looked both ways but was struck
when I dared to stumble.

PROVINCETOWN, MA

I stood near the pier but
not upon it   too unsettled
to walk closer to the water

let's say I could see the pier
and stood just where the road met
the sand that went directly to the water

I winced
though no sun was out and
the sky was a weary slate
and I was weary as usual

even the sand, dankly blanched,
knew only the water would hold
me and keep me and

I was afraid but I lived for that embrace
even more than I couldn't live
without it.

And we die.
        But
                that's not the point.
Power determines
                . . . I know.

I've lost my thought.

        Yes
        here it is:

Like magic we die   just as

        like magic we are born

but

        it's still hard in its way

        and the dying is harder.

Harder to take.

So why the preference?   To see another

        dead.
        To enjoy it with hands in a blue pocket?

    ~

                I love to see another's

breath in the cold air. To mingle my breath with another's

into that blue, as if we were smoking from one generous pipe.

Our swirl of a small cloud mirroring the cumulous world above

where we imagine

             the so-called good go when *their* breath stops.

But

          all breath travels out and up   disperses

                         and

cannot be followed.

ALRIGHT, I AM THE ONE YOU PREFER DEAD

. . . and I will die   I will.

      So why the impatience? The joy with my death

in your sight   or

worse   pretending to not see who else has me in theirs?

It's a game?   It's a game!

Yes   I forgot how much so many love their games

        like men who demand to lead

          all dances

who won't tolerate being led to a bed

        or boardroom

      ever the hunter never the hunted

              of course.

I have no need to parry.

You want me dead   and I will be.

I don't need you to move the pieces.

      You like it when things just fall

into place.

I know mine—

And if you say you, no, you don't want me
                              dead

then where were you yesterday?

When I said "help."

THE QUIVER TREE

is recognized by few, and fewer
know its uses, but those who do . . .

I grew up on the Panhandle, you might say
in that dry space I choked and coughed and fought

for my life in gingham and long white collars,
pink lace socks and plaits—thick and dark and

growing straight from my head like stiff leaves—
stiff as the Llano acacia in arid places, as if to approximate

a sun in its pale, suffocating bloom.

Take Marvin Gaye. His father had no mercy. Paranoia does that. Mercy is spat like spinach between the teeth. It slips out in a pee stream. Those without it lose it by adulthood. Flatline. It is replaced by a thin-lipped smile of rage. And with mercy goes empathy. But Marvin wanted mercy so badly from a man who didn't have it to give, as if all he once had now rested in Marvin. Who wouldn't be jealous? To see your better self. To hear all that beauty wafting out of every car window sweet as cigarette smoke. I don't trust those who don't like the smell. Orthodoxy. That was the gun in his daddy's hand. It said *don't* this and *don't* that and the only goodness is to wither on your own vine. But how could a man in the flowering of his life, so much abundance, let it go? He needed. He lost. Lost to the one always praying who should have repented, whose sins (if there are sins) were all there to be seen as that bullet that set aside flesh. I imagine it differently. It soothes me to do so. Marvin spent in his father's arms after a cruel night. Envy replaced by pride in the son. His own wintry pride displaced by . . . love. See, even you can't stand such sentiment. So how much harder was it for Mr. Gaye on his high horse. Stomping down the seed.

to the worst in men. And in my mother.
Strangers love me best. Fearlessly.

There the odalisque lies, wondering why
I won't stand behind her. I'm on the divan.

I have witnessed a shift in the times, time's shift.
But not enough. My mother almost loved me.

She laid the pattern for my dresses and
my life. Invisible to most I walk ahead.

*

My friends do not share their affairs, but
I see too much to not know.

They use me to judge themselves but
I am no one's judge. They just aren't strong

enough to walk forward and keep walking.
Hesitant. They stop in the galleries and

stare at the nudes. Imaginations like tongues.
If a man asks me to slap him. I do.

Not every man needs such a reminder. But
I don't mind really. Reminding them.

History can't be shaken, brushed off.
It can only be . . . addressed. Where it lives

I go. Take my hand, I'll take you.
There, there. Every mammal cries.

I've seen it. Nothing can't be hurt.
You aren't looking hard enough.

I recognize myself.

How pedestrian of you

to not notice the signals. Blithely

crossing   the monochrome streets

of the newest civilizations with their

simple civilities. ~~How fortunate~~

I am in this moment where I can choose

to disappear,   ~~cease~~

~~to exist~~ among you. But why?

It is not that I am   impolite. I am not

afraid of a word. You say *black*

I say Blacker.   I have shown you

a tomato garden but you say savage.

I dislocate my

back, bend until

the back

of my   head

touches   my   heels,

until my reflection holds only what won't

be   feared

but

fearing—

You say   *savage.*

Yes.

I'VE BEEN THINKING ABOUT LOVE AGAIN

Those who live to have it and
those who live to give it.

Of course there are those for whom both are true,
but never in the same measure.

Those who have it to give are
like cardinals in the snow. So easy
and beautifully lit. Some
are rabbits. Hard to see
except for those who would prey upon them:
all that softness and quaking and blood.

Those who want it
cannot be satisfied. Eagle-eyed and with such talons,
any furred thing will do. So easy
to rip out a heart when it is throbbing so hard.

I wander out into the winter.
I know what I am.

I KNOW THAT MUSIC

Up above my head
  (Up above my head)
I hear music in the air
  (I hear music in the air)

—Sister Rosetta Tharpe

So when Sister Tharpe swings that guitar on her hips
I know what she's rockin' for—

I've been lost in that music, fell down
on my knees. Women in white gloves
wrapped me in a sheet, took me in their arms
and let me sway to their rhythms while I sobbed.

Some say the Lord had taken me.
My father was proud I "got happy in the church"
but I didn't speak in tongues. I had no visions.

I had my troubles, already too much for my young
and narrow shoulders. I've had my cross to bear
and the music,   the music took those planks,
and I was for a few moments free of the world,

and of you. It was no heaven, my heart
was racing too fast for that. Not serene. Nor joyous,
but weightless. I couldn't see your judgment.
My face was a lyric everyone was singing.
Is there a finer beauty?

When my father realized it was not the Lord
but something "else," he remembered his disappointment

in me. The way so many do when I am not
what they want, or the way they would have me be.

If I were possessed, it was by that blue note
that captures suffering and squeezes it like a maid's
dishrag. Slaps the water from the fiber against those hips.
That antimelody that knows you best and loves you even more.

. . . the county held a field and
the field held a farm . . .

. . . a boy held a hound by the collar
as the hound held a bone in its mouth . . .

. . . a crow caught the eye of the girl and
the girl held its gaze . . .

. . . a cage had held the crow until
the crow found the key,

which was to grow until the cage broke,
until the cage could not contain it

but by that time it was mad.

. . . the wings of a crow held the air as
the air held the crow   up . . .

. . . the girl did not hold in her screams
once the crow held her nape in its beak . . .

. . . a mother held a broom to break the hold
of the crow on her daughter . . .

. . . the caw had caught the mother's attention
and the cows a-ways down the road holding

cud in their maws, mashing, mashing,
placidly and slowly . . .

. . . the girl had seen the eyes of the crow
held madness but it was too late by then . . .

. . . the girl could not keep her legs under her
and the crow had seen the nap of her hair and

wanted tufts of it for the nest he would build
for himself.

. . . the bird buried in her nape its talons and
burrowed its beak into her nap, its head bent

at an angle as if to whisper through the strands
something important, so important into her ear and
he had the voice, he did, a crow can mimic others,
but what of meaning? She didn't know.

. . . the broom held the mother's fear, feathers, hair,
and spots of blood falling on the bird and the girl's back

until up it flew, then down it fell.

. . . men holding rifles shot the bird from the sky as,
head tilted, the girl watched the feathers fall black

against a sky as blue as it had been before, and remains.

. . . that bird had held on to its few fine moments like
a kind of hope: the treat of the air and the raven-haired girl,

her staring into him as if she had been caged once
herself and would, perhaps, understand.

I like a troubled man. I mean to say, if a man's in troubled waters I'll want to tread them. Poets, musicians, fucked-up thinkers, mean motherfuckers. Marriage didn't end the propensity. Give me a feral cat to bathe in the sink. To blow-dry and pet. My grandmother was a lover of people her whole life. A drifter on her back porch could eat her good food from a pie tin. Dust everywhere then but in her house. She said, *Honey, you gotta love peoples when they down.* I make pies and feed them to my husband. He won't let strangers near the flat. So I feed friends. I love until there's no love left. My friends lick the tin plate. I pick at the crumbs. Strangers leave a plate clean, love better, don't leave me to fall apart. I've parted the hair of my girlfriends with a lick of grease while Marvin Gaye heated the room alongside the straightening iron. Of course my best friend married my boyfriend. Of course my boyfriend shared my love letters. What did I expect? It's a mean world and there's no denying how bad things can get. Marvin's daddy shot him dead. I want to walk down the street, under the new trees in Detroit, and tell Marvin I understand. To let his daddy go. That—*trouble don't last* unless you hold on to it. But that's not true. Trouble is always. He knew that. You know that.

UNCLE SONNY

I went to the funeral.
I had neglected him.
Rarely called.
Rarely wrote.
He lived in Lubbock.
I didn't want to go there.
There were relatives
I no longer spoke to
who kept having children.
So many cousins
I couldn't remember all
of their names. Those names.
Harder to pronounce than mine.
I loved it when he visited.
Matching hat to toe.
A purple suit.
Purple shoes with a buckle.
A preacher.
A man of God since he was a little boy.
I was his "early Christian"
on a good day. His "pagan"
on a bad one.
He loved me as is.
As few have ever done.
He begged for my company.
I let him down.
As I have been let down.
But never by him.
He was dying on the black side
of a town with no black side.
Poor is poor. Except
for the racists. Who exist
with pride in Texas.

The nursing home smelt
like sour greens. Dandelions
gone bad. He didn't know me.
When I reached to hold him
he was frightened. I'd seen that
look before. I wondered
if my heart was breaking.
I don't know anymore.
It doesn't beat the way it used to.
It's been a long time
since I've heard from it.

BLESS THE KINDLING WORLD

Bless the kindling world
that straps its children
into armor then sets a wick

beneath their feet.
They splinter. How we splinter
them. Limbs stacked and spilling

into dump yards, into graves,
into glutted rivers of amber.
Bless children raised to be felled.

We drain the tears from their ducts,
shake down the fat from their bones
until, light as brushwood, they rise

like sparks that flicker briefly
then sputter to their end.
Bless the tinder world,

a victory garden of sticks
we cull to feed our flame,
of stones we keep at hand.

BROTHER OF SKULLS

A girl sits in the church of bones weeping for her brother
who ran toward the doors. The river, a white current of skulls.

She knows his teeth, their chatter. In the church she sorts a heap
of bones. She still hears the hacking. She takes an armload of skulls,

kisses the hair and remaining flesh. Some seem to be smiling
like he would have before the radio orders, days of skulls.

Arms like vines grow out and up from the heaps as if to beg
for alms, or mercy from the god of this Church of Skulls,

where a town became a sun-bleached dune in a rainy season,
where roots clamber densely over the altar; in and out of skulls.

Who ran through these doors? Before they were shut
the girl lay still, pretending death to save the skin of her skull.

The church become boneyard holds her brother
within its doors. Amalu the beloved, Amalu of skulls.

ROOM FOR ONE

I want an ancient room, one aged
into beauty by collapse, the vicissitudes
of seasons, like leaves ever turning.

Pale coats of paint laid down, then
lifted over time, peeling way to dust and
moth and rain spilling over the sills. Spiders

claiming their corners, building hammocks
of threads, fragile as I am now. I want

to lie down in a room that knows
me, mattress upon a stone floor worn
by feet that trod, clicked, stomped, padded
their way through years of hope, then disaster.

I'll sleep in the imprint of those soles, traces
of purposes long forgotten—as I am
already, below these low beams, swaddled

by faltering plaster, a dress of white,
all a ruin, within a ruin, within

OMNIVORE

Todos saben que vivo, que mastico . . .
(Everyone knows that I am alive, that I chew . . .)
                                        —César Vallejo

Rat—teeth to the wood, hoary masticator
of plaster, brick, plastic, and bone.

And you, goat—chomping, chomping
with your mouth full of grass and tin.

We have no argument. I know
the heart must bite to beat. I know

like the young know, everything
must be tasted. Everything:

carrot . . . carpet . . . flesh . . . I will gorge
on this life from sour tit to last supper,

until the fields of tomatoes despise me,
until the cupboard is bare,

until there is nothing left but dust,
then, finally, I will bite into that.

THE FISHERMAN SPEAKS AGAIN OF HIS DAYS

To fish
To know
                    their small mouths   the shimmering
the thrash within
                    the net
flick of the knife   fleck
                    of scales caught in a light wind
                                        to float briefly then fall

                    Who can smile truly looking back?

I was a fisherman   a man
of the water   of mud and its secret
            pockets
of the water and what shimmers below
      water as it cools the skin

I was a man of rivulet and the riven belly pouring out its quick life

                    I look forward   over the hills
                    as if forgiveness were within a secret

                                        valley

I was a fisherman
I had a wife
I had daughters I could feed
whose hands were plump as fish bellies
whose fingers were always jumping   dancing then

There was a storm
There was no other sign

I slipped in the boat
The waters spilled in   then

When I woke I was still a fisherman
but I was not where I had been

Past the boundaries there is always a price

I was a fisherman   I was not a fisherman
I was a spy that was not a spy
When the prong slid between my legs
no hands held it
        It was a water snake   perhaps
        it recognized me   perhaps
        I had ignored it on the other side
        in my life as a fisherman

Some I threw back

I had a wife who was not yet swallowed by a hungry bitterness
and daughters whose plump hands happily swatted at minnows

Torture: To wrench, to harrow

Inside my hands danced in front of my face then up toward a light
A song played in my right ear
        The perfect song for a day I could not enter

Outside my wife swam away
undulant as a strand of hair caught in the current

       Outpourings: phlegm   spit   blood: the waters of the body

I was a spy then
I was sent back
          home
          I was never a spy

I have been thrown back into the world with a hook in my mouth
My hands   jump at unexpected   times
                mocking   flapping

                With my feet in a tub I saw fish at my ankles
                They were my daughters come to save me
                        I reached for them but
                                they slid from my grasp
                                        Just a shimmer under the surface
                        their mouths convulsively mouthing:
                                goodbye   goodbye   goodbye   goodbye

                        Are you listening?

I said   I am not a spy
                                ask the fish
I said   I will spy for you
                                release me

                        Torture?
                                Tell me what it means
Home: phlegm   spit blood   the same
waters   the same thrashing   carp   a li ght thro ugh t he fin gers
a disenchanted snake rising to hiss
                                spy   spy spy   spy

I am not a fisherman   I was never
a spy   I said that   to get back home to you

thrown back into the world I am all the world there is
So come   let's walk toward the river
                        Let's see what the fish have to say.

THE LIE

The lie was told first to a friend,
a friend who would nod in agreement,
then to another friend who was ready
to do anything to bed the teller, though
the teller had no general interest in that.
The teller only wanted relief from the truth,
so the lie grew as suspicion and spread like
kudzu over the trees.

Ask about the lie and another will be told
until the truth is a woman's body under
a Puritan's stone. Of course, every dark body
is suspect. A body escaping into a night.
A body sinking into a lake edged by woods.
The lie wants to snuff out the claims
of the body. So a laughing father wraps
his charred souvenir back into his handkerchief,
the same one he uses to swipe his brow, while
his wife pretends disgust, while down the road
a cockless body swings without desire.

AND UPON THAT PALE HORSE, A PALER WOMAN

after K. Wylie

She wouldn't hear me over her own voice.
    A call that fell like a
       rasp
on my ears was the dunnock's call
       to others.
My sisters asked, *Is that a sword in her hand?*

My brothers saw Glory riding
a glorious beast that
    took their heads
before they could offer them up.
       My cries were dust.
Who wanted my dry plot of tears?
       Hooves moved through
the backyard, then through the back door—
    I put down my pen and stood,
         struck
by the blush of her breasts as she laughed.
       She never looked down.
A hoof broke my ribcage.
      Her hair flew in strands of fire, and
    smoke filled my nose and mouth, and
my friends keep asking,
      Don't you have a god?

~

When the pale horse comes again, I won't bend. I'll seek the eye of the
heaving thing that once and again rode ripshod over my unflinching
form. I was crushed for so long, but

I got back up, pulled myself back together like a marionette who has outlived the puppet master. I watched her leave taking everything that was once mine with her. Now, the scent of death rises rank from me. My teeth still strong as bones in my black gums.

But I now ride my own

dark horse.

Now, we'll see.

EMMETT, I SAID WAIT

for W. Coleman

1.
Dreams are only as
safe as the sleeper.
I'm careful
before sleeping
to press my lips
into a tight cross-stitch
so nothing, no nothing
slips out.
He pulls me into his
fleshy mouth, a wound
I dab with my cheeks.
I suck the red
tear in his face, my hands
are wings (wrapped 'round).
He looked—
like a hare that's been spied,
caught
in the trap of an eye.

2.
He was bold.
For a cut second
I believed I was dreaming.
We moved in cracked film,
sepia staccato:
his cheeks going gaunt,
the teeth shuttered by pursing
mouth moving into red bow
(with that lurid hint
of pink). Then the sound
he made
lifted the hem of my skirt.

I said,
"Can you believe that boy
put his black lips together
to make that nasty sound?"

It was a question,
not an order.
I did not say
take him to that river.
I did not say
lay him on Isaac's stone.
I wanted to get home
to take this crinoline off,
to lie alone for a moment
with my hands
doves upon my breasts
before husking the corn,
before chicken in hot grease
poppin' my throat.

3.
Dreams are no safer
than the sleeper.
I recall him so
savage, but feel strange—sick
and soft even in this
position:
like a finger slicing its way
through new butter, or
the steamy bread
being broken.

I said *wait,*
they heard me,
I said *wait.*

By morning
my hair is disheveled.

I rush to the mirror
without making a sound,
pee, and arrange myself.
Put on my face
before starting coffee.

So what,
they said,
"Those boys ask for trouble,"

even now
with the magazine
years old,
the crack in his face
is a question mark.

4.
There were always boys
in town,
knees peeking through
threadbare pants,
elbows dangling
from unstarched sleeves
like dusty ribbon licorice.
I can see them through
my lashes,
over my rouge.
I look down, weigh them
with my glances.
They don't dare look up.

5.
His skin
against the eggshell
coffin silk
does not contrast
the way one might imagine.
He is pale as a honeydew

split upon a rock.
The glossy pages can't picture
how brown he was that day—
only how given to ashy white
he is now.

6.
Wait: before I wake
I mount his head,
press it into the fork
of my legs, the tricky
friction of my maneuvers
and his limber neck.
His hairs tight, embraced,
clinging by strands.
His haunches are slim
branches yielding.
I whistle through my nose
as I sleep, under covers
I snore in flaring passions.
When I come,
we are on the bank,
wet from the running
water,
bruised by bottom
stones.

I said *wait.*
Those boys hanging
out in town ought to have
known better. Somebody
should have told him.

7.
Who was he?
Even now
with the magazine
shut and crisp,

the crack in his face
is a question.

8.
I smile into his slender
throat, say,
don't you want some of this.

Dreams are dangerous
as the tongue
flicks along the channel of
a flat ear, shell shaped
as if it had just washed up
on a bare strip of sand,
sweet throb of meat
still inside.

He is silent.

I place my index finger
where his mouth was,
it sinks into the hole,
Hush now, hush,
I know, I know.

THE MARSH KING

And you who have not borne the open ocean,
stand at the lakeshore, among the rushes.
Days of dreaming—a black fin breaking
the water, a pair of dolphins arcing
silver from the waves. You are a fisher,
an explorer, a captain of men.

And while the orange-toothed nutria chews
the starched root, you, master of the marsh
bank, build ships of paper
and push them out to sea.

WITHOUT END

There is no final poem, just as
there was no original poem, and
if there was a tree that held a knowledge
of good and evil then we have done nothing
with that knowledge, moving back and forth
between the two, perplexed as sparrows
in a storm batting their small heads against
windows they don't see. The poem
is betwixt and beyond, within and out,
not the apple eaten, but the planets
themselves the apple and core, and we
the hungry, open, O—

READING NERUDA AT 2:00 A.M.

Boulders of the mountain—
teeth in a whale's mouth?

I recall it all wrongly. My dreams
have muddled the language the translator
spent years translating—
a gift of the tongue, a red bow.

Salt of the Pacific—
talc on a lover's back?

You want to read Neruda aloud by the street-
light that intrudes through the frayed curtain.
I say I am too sleepy—
You pick up *100 Love Sonnets*
sigh majestically and begin, *#1*

In my dreams cliffs line the shore—
knees and elbows on the pale sheets—

A woman's laughter as she guts a fish—
a magenta bird's call: agent of longing and despair.

After a night spent in Isla Negra
you remain asleep as your lips close then part
as if sucking a lime or a stone,
while I wake hungry for

flesh and pomegranates—
that don't blush for me but for us and the sea.

What the cooling air expects
as the day's rigid heat gives
way to the wind like the back
yielding to a warm palm. An imprint
is left. The hand is felt
long after it is lifted, and the river
has swallowed the sun and in its depths
that heat ripples the floor. But
where I swim belly-up, relief
is the promise of night running
the body's length and I am neither cold
nor frightened by the cold, just anticipating
the sharp stars, the wide-eyed beasts.

THE WINTER KINGDOM

1. *Ice*

The Winter Kingdom is bordered by a lake
a forest

fields of dead wheat   blanched
as the snow under which they rest

One imagines horses   but
wheels have already replaced hooves

and brick has given way to pavement
These too lie under the white counterpane

2. *The City*

The City is the jewel
of the Kingdom   like a diamond on the finger

or the first piece of coal   lit in the grate
ready when white-ashed to heat a white room

I pull a coat from the closet   black
with blacker velveteen roses   a statement

against the white
stark as the   mole   on my eyelid

Other coats join me in step
We walk head down

hands in pockets   boots sloshing
toward whatever it is that matters

We speak slowly   if at all
and make only small gestures

gestures and poems
When there is music   we dance in rounds

We play the instruments of our fathers
and their fathers before them

Ancient songs on ancient strings
Every season it will snow   and a season may last

more than half our lives
                              so we sing to the ice   to the ice—

   3. *Snow*

A girl became lost in the field of dead wheat

By the time she was found
the sweet fat of youth had congealed

enough to be plucked
by the starlings

This story keeps us   inside
the borders

And   the lovers who secreted themselves away
in the forest, only to be taken by bears

        this too keeps us from straying
        Boats may sink upon the dark lake

        deep as the snow is high
High as the mountains   the snow

When we travel it is to or from the City of the Winter Kingdom

The Winter Kingdom has *always* been
a man says to me as if it were true

What would it serve to disagree?

I pull up my collar against the cold
and nod
            though I can't say   why.

There stands a blue-
shingled house with
white trim. A bare
yard where tumble
small tumbleweeds.

The kind of house
where a pink poinsettia
(half its leaves already dead)
might soldier on through
an easy winter.

There's still hope?
But it is thin as the slats
of cheap blinds.

Mouth to saucer,
saucer to mouth,
a cigarette for what
it's worth. The music
of a vinyl chair cracking.
That's right. Sometimes
we settle for whatever
doesn't harm.

    The linoleum is mopped. TV dusted.
    The cabinet, with its canned green beans.

Wise ass. Owl-eyed. Taker of flesh. Forest dweller. Spoon in her apron. Stirrer of pots and men. Alone and beside. Healer, some say. Rumor-drawer. Never-teller. Too dark for this. Too heavy for that. Tendencies toward both. Always something simmering. Taster. Some say, *She ain't shit.* Her mouth gapes. Her teeth gap. She's got no eyelids but always looks like she has something to say. Like she wants something. She says, *Give it here.* She's a feral heifer. She says, *So the fuck what?* and, *What the fuck are you looking at?* She says, *Get the fuck out of my face.* Volcanic. Always hot. Ready to blow. Owns herself. No man's slave. Some kind of diva. She says, *Get it, girl.* Her third eye's always itching. Ask, Who does she think she is? She's unclear. Muddy. Sees no need say it twice. You know who she is. Other-side-of-town woman. Wears a slip on the front porch. Will tell you it's always summer where she is. Sweats as much as her glass of iced tea. As the liquor she tops it off with when she's inclined. She's always inclined. No master but God and not even then. Blasphemous. She's hard work. She works hard for every little thing. Whose welfare? She taking care of you. She say, *It's an exchange.* So why you fuckin' with her if you don't wanna fuck. Night woman. Keeps her curtains closed. She's always been . . . She doesn't demand much. Gets more than she asks for: split lip, broken glass, a man's knuckles, a woman's ring. She a wiseass. She read too much. That's her problem. Book learning. She tucks them under the bed. Dust and hair. She comb her hair sometimes. Washes it the old way. Creek water and witch hazel. She goes on anyway. Standing in the doorway. Waiting to see what you gone do. She slips the pink of her tongue over the fish before she fries it. She wanna know what she's getting. When you're done, she's the bitch that's done with you. She'll tell you herself. She know who she is. She's unraveled the night. The town wants her dead.

rose from the floor of a valley.
It woke me. A lowing from the low country.
From the bottom of all things, from some place
I may never rise from, it rose. As if something forgotten
was at last found, or what was long neglected   awakened.
Something under untrapped. And the sound rose as a needed *yes,*
yes . . . It ascended like a hell-bent *ever.* The sound rose true without fear
or embellishment. Unmuffled. A sound that cannot understand a lie
and so cannot produce it. And though I thought I couldn't fall farther,
I fell to my knees before the sound. Humbled by such truth.
A moan. A wailing. I cannot say how long it lasted. It was all
and whatever it had to be. It was the same sound you uttered
in your sleep and would utter now if only you were brave enough.

THAT CAT

smiled that small-mouthed smile and
like a tabby I lapped it up. I have a lap
cat. He sleeps whatever way I sleep.
If I am on my right side, he moves to
his right side. If I am on my back, he lies
on his back. He cries for me when I leave.
He makes dinner when I'm hungry. God
knows I love a cat that hungers for me.
But what cat won't I pick up if it hasn't had
milk in a while. Won't I just lay out a bowl?
Cup the palms of my hand and offer it up?
My cat purrs in his sleep and in his sleep
spreads out my hair like a pillow to purr into.
I've never known a cat so comfortable
with a human. Oh! Did I tell you?
Not everyone knows I'm human. That I
walk on two legs unless I'm getting down
on four (but that's another story, that's
a wolf's tale). I am human and woman
but am often mistaken for a bear or taken
for a beast. I frighten the rabbits. I am
wickedly pecked by the dumb chicks, the
fucking thin-billed geese who can't chase
me from the yard. One day a man's gonna
mistake me for a coyote and shoot my ass.

And what did I expect going back
"down" South? I could walk the side-
walks. I could look anyone in the eye.
I could swim in the pools. I could, I could,
I could, I could . . . and I ate at fine restaurants
where the chef greeted me and asked me
how my meal was, and I ordered a simple
plate at a simple diner and no one looked
up any more than usual, and the beaches
welcomed me, and the chains of hotels
on those beaches, and not one person
said, "nigra," and did you think I wouldn't
say it here? I went back after saying I would
never go back, after a childhood lost
to adult madness without a sword or a gun,
without a bitter word or rude glance,
like a fractured saint, like a saint with every
bone fractured, I walked with a limp,
I smiled with half my teeth and I was
ready to die in the war begun before
I was born. But I could not find the battle-
field. And the field my mother would have
worked as a child was a parking lot. And I sat
between the lines and cried for what
I would never have, justice.
And the tanks within me rusted, and
the bombs imploded in what was left.
Now, I know what I saw was a lie,
and what you see is a shell.

THE WHEEL OF THE BUS: A FICTION

Ms. Parks at the Henry Ford Museum

The bus made new, yellow, no, white, *Yes*—moves down the blacktop (cue the organ, fingers darkening the ivory). She hovers like an oversized sparrow, remembers that that day was not extraordinary, that she was not extraordinary (how she once shook like a common rag doll in a mugger's embrace). And her relatives—like any other's—not particularly special. She leaves through the rusted gate, hears music, no, a horn. She sees a sidewalk below. A familiar curb? The bus stands polished, illumined as if it had never been driven, all the seats made equal. *Mother?* she muses. *Mother of Manners. Mouth of Doves. Mother. Mother mother mothermother motherfucker.* She will tell him what she was really thinking. She can't remember what she really thought. *Pig? Yes—you little potbellied pig.* She moves closer to the roof of the bus. *Shut your filthy mouth. SHUTITJUSTSHUTITSHUTIT.* She waves the index finger of her right hand at the bus, moving quicker than she could before she died. In pantyhose, sensible shoes, and glasses she lands neatly on the roof of the bus, adjusts her bun. *Blake, get out of there! For goodness' sake*, she thinks, *why was I so good so good so very very good? Blake!* He too is behind a gate, his fingers white-gripped around the bars. His is a bird's-eye view. A guinea fowl. He has been waiting for this moment. He hears her rage, as he heard it then, but now she is so much louder. He screams, *Ma'am, I'm sorry, so sorry, it was my boss.* Rosa kicks out the front window of the bus. The bus is a museum. The bus has no engine. *Mother of Muggers.* She kicks in another window of the bus moving nowhere, moving through the streets of Montgomery. She eases into a front seat. *Come out, coward!* He doesn't cry anymore, the way he used to when his wife wasn't watching. It is her, *Mother of Movements, Madre of Martirio* whose pipe he must smoke. The bus backfires, alive now with the smell of fumes, pressed trousers, patent leather purses, and paint. She wipes the blood from her ankles, smoothes her lap with gloved hands. Stares at the empty driver's seat.

RELEVANCE

Which I'd provide if we shared more
than fear. And sometimes not even that.
What can I say to help you
see where I'm coming from? To help
you not . . . and what use is it?
I haven't given up but have so little left
to give. Miłosz says, "Listen," and I do.
But it takes a bowed head. Nature
is so much more than I can stand but
its indifference makes more sense to me
than yours. Why play on the beach? Now,
of all times. But, who's to say what another
needs. I have been left so long alone . . .
This is not at all how I meant to say this.
Some things take time to say. Sometimes
the cure is disaster first. Sometimes silence.
Being still as a kind of humility. As a kindness.

IV

AN UNKINDNESS OF

The crow that strafed my nape as a child had
himself been squeezed into a cage and kept
from others. Crows go mad alone, and
there I was looking at him looking at me and
in that hesitance I knew he didn't know
whether to fly into my arms or at me.
He bloodied my neck, then flew off. Those are the bones
of the matter. Crows have always been drawn to me
so I thought they were my spirit animal as feral
as my parents, unwilling to meet my needs but there.
I wanted a friend. My father said, "Never."
            And I have heard ever so many times since—
I don't believe in forever, but ravens,
unlike crows, can abide as only one. Though two may travel far
together, they can be cruel.
                              I wanted to be away.
Leave my parents themselves. I had siblings, weren't they enough?
Would it have been so wrong to leave me to my own devices
instead of keeping me only to be disappointed? I cannot deny the animals
that haunt me. But with humans I make my peace with solitude.

LANDSCAPE

(West Texas Panhandle, Winter 2018)

1.   hasn't changed. The mountains

remain treeless and full of their invisible life,
like the javelina in the backyard dark as its own
shadow under the thick prickly pears, unseen
but heard grunting, barking, rooting.

Where did everyone go? The ones
whose eyes I could not look into?
The ones I got off the sidewalks for?
Who are *these* people?

Inside what would have been an old shed
a few years back is a café. All the ink-stained
writers, writing. No long guns. No shotguns.
A mistletoe wreath on the door. No one
cares that I'm here, or if they do, they have
the sense to pretend indifference. Another kind
of disappearing. I catch the old accent
in an aging body desperately trying not to age,
but the face betrays the slim jeans. Yoga body.
Time bends us. I know yoga won't undo
its lessons. Now, the corrugated tin doesn't rust
the way it used to. Money being damned
and shifted ruthlessly like waterways in the West.
What was a sign of poverty is now a sign
of privilege. The corrugated tin of the house
by this café is a deep pink, like the lining
of a brown woman's inner lip. On my table
is a spiderless cactus. I can walk any sidewalk,
look up, wave or smile without being slapped.

2. In a white car I cross the tracks

    back and forth and back and forth and . . .
    because I can . . .

3. What I remember

    you would not believe.

4. I had forgotten how deceptively subdued

    the desert palette. How the sun blanches
    me into you.

MY DOLLS WERE JUST THAT

(West Texas Panhandle, Winter 1971)

1.
    Dolls.

To think those eight blond heads

(four on either side of mine) might protect

me. Those nights terrors that presaged

later terrors equally dark would not be stopped

by their hard plastic heads, those chewed pink scalps.

Why would they

save my body? Brown as it was,

animate, soft.   They didn't love me.

I loved them.

I brushed their hair and they expected

me to. I rubbed their legs between my

own but only I came. They were pretend

but I never pretended. I privileged them

and served them

tea (and cookies, when I could sneak them

into my bedroom, which my mother

insisted I keep clean and crumb-free).

I was crumbling and my dolls could not

stop it. They sat up straight as plastic

soldiers on the pillows

as I held vanilla wafers to their mouths.

2.
Cotton candy.

The old woman (from Georgia?

some southern place)

touched my hair at the café and said that

and I obliged, saying, *Yeah, more cotton*

than wool. Then I immediately thought

of the flaxen hair of my old dolls now

in the basement of memory, which I washed and cut

with my tiny hairdresser fingers

while I waited for my breasts to grow

straight out and my own hair to grow

straight down.   I'm losing the thread

of my recollections, so you probably can't

follow me. Yes, rabbit holes. There were so many

back there in West Texas. And so many

Alices. Alices everywhere. So popular.

One year there was a rabbit infestation.

But I've told you about that. I didn't

tell you how many girls followed them

down

down

down

I am repeating myself. I wanted a rabbit

too. A fluffy white one with a pocket watch.

There were wild hares and . . .

some were rabid, but I didn't believe that.

Tens of thousands of them with their

long ears and raggedy bodies.

I was so

drawn to them. No one cared what hole

I fell down. I looked under the bed

every night. So scared. And held my dolls

close. Squeezing them into my ribs

as if they could ward off whatever

came for me. And when it did,

they were nowhere to be found.

MEAT EATER

No, I won't apologize for that.
Though I may stop, because
chewing is harder without two molars.
But the protein I need can't be had
another way. I prefer the meat of goats.
That they die with dignity (if there is dignity
to be found) and their lives be green and good.
It is *possible* I will turn to greens alone,
let the kitchen of my youth
inhabit my kitchen now: kale, collards,
turnips—I eat oxtails with yams. Ham with peas.
Don't need to eat my chicken in Paris.
The best cooks are in Mississippi. Though
I still won't go. I've seen enough of
South Carolina too. I miss raccoon.
Though I hated the taste so it must be
my grandfather I miss. And when I eat
ribs my father comes to mind and
we are close for a moment. Is it worth
the sacrifice of animals. I can't answer that
right now. I'm picking my teeth.

GOAT HEART

See the goat? Desperately lithe
on the mountainside. Climbing higher
but beyond the cold whip
of the winds. The creature is
focused on its destination. We know
the end will be sad. The end may
end it. But a goat sings on
the unmarked trail of its travails.
A goat sings until its throat gives out.
Until its legs grow brittle. Without
a cane or help. With no one listening.
A goat sings until its lungs grow blue and
its heart plops right out of its mouth onto
the hard floor from the sheer exertion of trying
so hard to be heard so far below, in the valley
that thinks nothing of it. Doesn't
even know it is up there.

I AM THE ONLY ONE I KNOW WHO CAN COOK THEM, AND MY GRANDPA DID, WAS IN FACT KNOWN FOR SEVERAL COUNTIES ROUND FOR HIS WAY WITH A POT, SO

After hearing the great poet read
about chitlins I cried in my car for an hour without
succor. I had said, *I "get" your poem and not many of us will*
bite into chitlins anymore and you and I are covering similar
material in our poems . . . but the poet heard a "local" and
was busy signing books while I was busy being embarrassed.
I was no yokel, but there I was with my sun-mottled face,
and my memories of ham-hocked collards and the cloy
of cornbread and yams like a cologne coming off my skin,
betraying my background of jukes and long-horns, Sulfer8,
Christmas coon, the rusting hoes and spades. But
I'm the kind of goat that means to get up the god-
damned mountain no matter what howls or rips into me
so years later when the great poet, having got to know me,
whispered, *I'm gonna take you to my secret BBQ joint*,
I knew I was not off the mark, that we held in common
a kind of heat: brine from the mason jar, Hot Jim, whatever
slides easily from the bone. And anyone Texas-born like myself
knows the secret joint is the for real god-almighty sauce
where there's mud on the floor and the pork smells like the lover
you wish you had (or do). Where there's a fan overhead and
it ain't coolin' nothin' down, and you know your uncle would love the place
so he don't need to know. Neither does your daddy.
Where, as you spoon up peppers, your tongue remembers itself
and the vernacular you let go; that real talk climbs your leg
like a good bitch lost to a hound, or down your spine
like a red ant under the collar, and then you come back to yourself,
know yourself know for the earthy motherfucker you are,
ain't that right though?
          You'll leave this place stained

and smoked and grateful you stayed so long where nobody blinks
when a bit of brisket is spit accidentally through the gap of a smile,
where no one is embarrassed by what they must eat, or love to.

1.
As I fell, bits of this and that caught
in my hair, more cotton
candy than wool, and if wool, the wool
of a day's old lamb, thinner and whitening,
into its sugared mass went whatever found its way
to the ground or had been ground under:
a brittle piece of leaf, thorns
of the althorn, tears of feathers from the swallows
as they burst from the althorn, blades of winter
grass, inedible berries, the bitter tip of sticks,
a blond strand, then another . . .
then a hairball of straw, cactus spines, sun-blanched
blossoms of the prickly pear. I became my own tumble-
weed of detritus and desire, my own perpetual roiling
of hair ever growing out like a kit's whiskers
even as I fell down, drawing motes of dust—

I had followed him. It was on me. No one
saw me fall. Everyone else was looking elsewhere.
I was known for not being known. For all intents
and purposes—
                    invisible
and he was so furtive, almost sincere in his urgency,
constantly checking his waistcoat, slicking back
his hair in a way that said *take a good look at my tongue*
pink as the inside of his lips, as it slipped over his palm
then his palm slipping over his fine fine hair.
He kept looking from side to side, but no one was looking
back at him. They were doing whatever the mundane
morning demanded. Cocky bastard—

2.
He didn't know I was following him. That's how
invisible I was. I once dated a man who thought he was
a ninja once. One date. I said, *Naw, nigga, you ain't a ninja.*

3.
Still, he was a trickster, that hare. Tall enough to
appear to be standing straight from a distance.
An elongated torso on enormous feet that meant
absolutely nothing except
he loped and couldn't find good shoes. I thought
he was a man despite my eyes. I should have known,
considering how easily he startled. Roiled into a temper
over everything: a cool breeze, a warm wave, a dance
of dandelions, a bird appearing on a walk, my silence,
my chatter. Damn. What wouldn't scare him?

4.
When I hit the first bottom, the false
bottom, there was a cat waiting for me.
He took me on the real drop.

Hell. That cat was a trickster too.
Often since, I wonder how good they were, or
how easily I can be fooled. I knew the hole
was there. I followed that hare down.
I would have followed him anywhere.

Was the same with my father.
My mother made sure I knew she didn't want me
going anywhere with her. "Stop following me," she said.
I stopped.

5.
Aren't rabbits beautiful? All that shiver and rustle.
All that bite and hustle.

6.
You are wondering how I lived to tell the tale.
How I got back? I grabbed the end of a crow's
tail. But how could feathers carry my weight?
I fell again. I'm clumsy. *Foolish little girl.*
I have an ugly face when I cry, so no one stops
to comfort me. I barrel along like a boy with a hoop.

7.
I can't get all of this shit out of my hair.

I don't have food. If I abducted children like that,
here in the bush, what do they eat?
—Joseph Kony, leader of the Lord's
Resistance Army, Uganda (2006)

In a black car, the big man in sunglasses—
rode hungrily through the streets. Medals clanging,

gleaming in the ever-present sun, like a sun god
he smiled and blinded the onlookers. Note

how round he was, round as the sun itself, and always
so hot, sweating, roasting under collar and all

of those medals. He demanded tribute
and daily rose to claim it.

When the big man bit into a fatless thigh
he was not on four legs, he strode on two.

He himself would say, *Do not call me an animal,*
I am so much more than that.

Who hunted for the big man? Who charred
the questionable meat? That day he plucked

a child's pinky from a golden plate and ran it over
his wet lips. Chop licker, bone sucker—

why blame the jackal? Don't put it in *his* mouth.
Nor the lion's, whose teeth were bloody, true,

but he was resting in the shade of a stunted fig tree.
No,

it was the big man who gnawed the knuckles.
Like a skinny man does now, three decades later.

The skinny man, whose wiry frame holds even more
than the big man's fat belly could. And *his* palate

is delicate: lips, tongue, the nape of the neck.
Who has learned anything

if not from the big man?
How to raise an army from dust?

How to split a small skull
using only your thumbs?

How to convince the eaten that they are not
being eaten?

the leafless tree   *dead tree*
the greening grass   *Easter grass*
the blue flowers   *blue flowers (are you stupid?)*
all drinks   *cold drinks*
all soda   *cola*
the bees   *just bees (you ask too many questions)*

from this I grew a vocabulary of sparse images,

that man just down the road
that girl at the market

where a last name stood for many, for
an understood history

one of the Bowie sisters
one of the Bowie daughters
Mr. Jackson, who sells that sugarcane

Instead of the names for things
cornflower
lupine
I listened for the particularities of how things are said
hersh
erl
breafas
(less a language than a knowing)
opens a trail to my younger self
with a tongue so languid every word
was feathered inside
a shhh or phhh

toofbrush
  Caphedral

I would accidentally whistle as if happy
even when sorrow burrowed under
my skin like a tick in the plump of an arm,

So I was hushed when I spoke my small discoveries
at the dinner table. People wondered when I'd grow out of it:
speaking out of turn.

all fish   *catfish*
meat   beef
chicken   chicken

from sparse description I grew
an imagination   filled in the gaps
      "the man who sold cane syrup from the tin"
      "the Bowie sister who held my head against her ample bosom
      when my grandmother died"
      "the dead tree that lets me know where the property line ends"

but *the blue flowers* remain the blue flowers
that were my mother's favorites, the ones she knew by smell
that good smell

WHY I DON'T WAIT

Because I used to and
now the years have gone by
and some of them without me.

And my passions have drifted
or heightened and either way
they have my attention.

Because there are some who don't
mind and will meet me where I am.

And those who simply like the right now
no matter what the right now holds
and there is danger going back, remember?
And what is there ahead if our feet slip now
because we refused to see where we stand?

Look, there is a summer cottage where a couple sleeps
without food. Stolen shelter. And there
is an old man who won't see his family again
and can't recall their faces not because his mind won't
let him, but because he refused to see his family
and now, can't. So many cruelties in the now.

And if we lose this moment? We lose our balance,
the promise inherent in the well-worn waking hours.

THE COMPANY OF WOLVES

All we like sheep have gone astray . . .
                                    —Handel's *Messiah*

You found me where the forest was black
like broken piping sticking out from cement.
And the ash that fell like snow
when the factory was torn down,
and the snow itself, present half the year.
There were no coyotes but cats just as feral
and mad (as any abandoned being becomes).
That year the rats froze into the ice,
and quicker, hungrier rats ate off their heads
that poked just above the ice-line, leaving their bodies
to be clearly seen in eternal struggle.
The sight disgusted you who walked the alleys,
you loved to walk off the edge, so there
was nothing I could say. And I wanted to
warn you about the wolves. But you
did not fear them, you feared for me.
Cities like ours are as full of wolves
as dogs. They leave no footprints. There
is always more than one. They can smell a sheep
like me. And I can't tell a wolf from a neon sign.
I move toward the brilliant lights, which charm
like the glinting watch the hypnotist swings
back and forth. I will embrace any bright-eyed creature
and if not for you, lay it on my pillows. A wolf can
pretend otherwise until you are asleep.
That is how the granny was taken
in that old story. She took the beast in and let it
sleep beside her. The only thing it left was her cap,
which he put on his own head. So believe me,

the difference between a wolf in the forest and one
on the street is that one lives on the street. The streets
I walk when I am restless, wearing red, and wanting
to make friends. How many times have you taken me
out of a sharp-toothed mouth just before
I was swallowed whole? Why do you think
I follow your staff and come only when you call?

THE SHORE

In a nondescript hotel in South Texas, I thought
I had fallen in love with a couple. There in the dim

hallway with rugs that were clean enough
but darkly patterned to hide the stains so who knows,

her back was against the wall, her arms up and around
his neck. He was bent down to kiss her, to press

his body into hers. Their bodies were fluid, two waves
not crashing but moving through each other—

I watched them from the other end of the hallway,
surprised to see them. I halted. Doesn't another's passion

make us want? They never saw me. I didn't stay long
and stayed silent. She was not his wife. His love

was palpable. His hands were tender not quick. Slow
not furtive   That press.

I have been a witness to such passion more than once,
more than most. On a nondescript street in Manhattan,

in a nondescript restaurant whose patrons—too young
to value discretion or quiet—spoke in loud voices

and fell drunkenly over the tables. I saw a friend through
the oversized windows. The street lit by random lights.

He drew her up into his body. She was no friend of mine.
She followed me to follow him. She found him

and drew his face down to hers. They kissed in a way
that said they had kissed many times before and

perhaps it had been a long time. The kiss was long
and deep and I ate my steak au poivre bloody under sauce

and waited for them to finish, for him to come back
to the table after rushing out "to take a call."

They never saw me watching. Didn't even look up.
He swept her up as if his entire body longed

for a certain kind of completion. Her hair so like his mother's
he might have cried into it. Where is the shame

in that? She was not his wife. I am not his judge.
I was on the shore, only a witness to the oceanic:

dangerous, tidal, reckless, and always.

NOUVEAU SLIM

Some are convinced if I simply practice yoga,
if I'd just consider it, I could be white, American
white. The small of my spine would uncurve,
straighten, as would my teeth. And the gap
of my teeth would close as a gap between my thighs
magically opened without me having to spread
my legs except upon a thin mat next to another
doing the same. In pants like another skin, and
that is the point. American yoga. The great equalizer.
As if my breasts will stop swinging apart as
those of the women of my line tend to do,
our nipples under by thirty whether we nurse or not.
As if my belly will flatten into some sign
of discipline and my self-denial taken as a sign of class here
on this *free* Vermont border where I have lost
my appetite even as I long for brisket and ribs
and collards and kale stewed the way the poor
stewed them before the wealthy decided they wanted
that too. And what's not to love here: the air,
the light, the houses older than ships. I can't
keep anything down but me. Where I am free
to be anything but in this body which is this skin,
but I don't just miss brown people, I hunger
                              for round people—
the body uncorseted by male design. The body roiled
with its curated appetites, content in stillness and
in its security having at last stopped its reaching.

There is a sister whose voice is gentle as a lullaby. A lulling. Even when angered, she won't yell. A particular upbringing that eschews the loud, though such a woman can be found embracing those whose voices swell in the streets. Perhaps less saintliness than a vicarious expression of her own rage? frustrations? Drawing the brawler, the harsh, and violent close. The softness embedded in her accent. An oiled woman. Pink lipstick on her brown lips. A woman who pulls biscuits from the oven on a Saturday. Bathwater woman. Sweet liquor in a white cabinet woman. I have found this woman in Tennessee. In Texas. In Alabama. In Mississippi. And clung to her. *Darling*, and *Dearest*, and *Hush, honey* on the tongue. Not silence but delicacy. A blue slip in the drawer. A breeze through the oak leaves. Cuss and she won't shush you, she'll laugh and take you inside. Feed you cake, brush out your damp hair, pull you onto her lap, draw the cedar from the wound.

EVERYWHERE AND HERE TOO

(leaving Asheville, North Carolina, again)

I would like to say the wind doesn't move through me,
that I don't respond to such things. That I don't stare at a field
of flowers or pole beans or even the ubiquitous corn. That
I don't feel the flatness of land with relief and want to run
and run and run across it the way I want to cry in the woods,
to cry without stopping because I can't imagine how someone
might escape through them. Because I know I am descended
from those who couldn't escape. Every place sets my teeth
on edge. I take it all in like needles like air whipped up
my nostrils as it rounds the corner of a brick building,
like a thumb in my mouth and honey from the jar
on the end of it. The righteous and the wrong. All
of it enters "the way bells enter" the waiting ear on a
Sunday morning, or the birds that wake me when I am
sleeping by the window or the moan of the neighbors
or my own. How can you strike the balance when you can't
separate yourself from anything or anyone—I am not safe
anyplace, and no place can save me. Just look what the mountains
have done to me. Exactly what the city did—and then some.

CANZONE IN BLUE, THEN BLUER

There wasn't music as much as there was
terror, so the music became as much a
part of the terror as the terror it-
self with the swell of the arpeggio building and
breaking, building and breaking, upon the shores
of you. Your shores washed slowly away but
not slowly enough, you still feel it, every grain
of sand a note going under, bluing the
body, granular and wet. This has happened
before. You weren't special. You belonged to
no group of concern any more particular
than another. But the music has become
you. The hurt coming out, from your open mouth, could
open a grave. Let every done-wrong haint throw
its head back and groan. Not done wrong as in some-
body loved left, somebody is always left,
but done wrong as in someone who deserved to live
as much as anyone else but died by another's hands
or neglect or the indifference of someone
who cared less or just not about you. And you sang
like you cried until the music of leaving,
of long gone became you. Does it matter how
many strings? It only takes one to make this
music. But let's say it was the sound of
a choir that accompanied the run of
blood down a leg. Let's say a violin sped
its notes down the side of a neck, a tirade
of pricks. Or a high C from a voice thrown sharp
as the pieces of skull a bullet through the
head would leave. Or the river, the river rush-
ing cold and rock bottomed, with its own furious
song carries you with it, sings you right over
the falls. That is when terror is not blue but bluer,

blue as capillaries bursting from an eye,
blue as the vein under this razor, blue as
the skin beat so far it breaks into song, a
song like this. And I've sung this so many times, dear,
my voice has almost given way, and I'm so scared.

In the care of my friends I have been made
to bend and bray and I cried and walked the sidewalks. I cried
and did not understand. Nor did they understand. What I wanted—
to be forgiven my faults—but I was given a hair shirt
and the burden of a tongue that slurped from any given bowl
and flapped in a futile manner. When I spoke they heard screeches and
guttural moans when I spoke. They said, *What?* They mocked me. My friends
knew the mule I could be. Only they, they said, could
tame my stubborn will. I was so often on my knees
I began to doubt my own footing. Brought so low
by claims of love. Sometimes they held sugar cubes
to my mouth. Sometimes I was so grateful
I licked their proffered hands.

THE WORLD CONTRACTS

—Adam Zagajewski

Sip a sweet cordial and the lonely stars grow closer,
lean forward, so unlike biting into a lemon
all pith and acid. Bite into that and
on the other side of the city a man will yell,
What the hell's in my eye?
Like yesterday, I saw the smoke of a fire
from the highway and I couldn't figure the miles.
It seemed close to my flat so I drove faster and
faster to save it, my home, from the flames,
flames I knew were below the smoke, but
when I got there, there was no fire,
just smoke wafting from the belching incinerator
ten miles further on. Still, the smoke *was* there
with its stink of waste. What is distance
but the leap from womb to luminescence? From
light to shade again. I toast the gazelle
whose flesh nourishes the lion I watch
on television. The lion is so close I fear it
but don't turn away. What difference is there
between birth slap and cry? Between
our eating and any other grind? I go out
into the night and throw up my arms
as if to pull toward me every unknown thing.

MOAN SOFT LIKE YOU WANTED
SOMEBODY TERRIBLE

—Carl Sandburg

if it comes to pass, the would-be politician, or the lover,

said what was never meant, and is now distant

as those moments your desire swirled about you

like new snow, cold and brisk and enlivening, remember—

it was you feeling adrift, misunderstood, calamitous, and

alone, you, dear, who needed until the need grew into a rally, a rant

of promises now unpromised—

and the night is a hand slid over your mouth. Demanding

your silence. It surprised you, the shift, the sudden denial,

the awkward indifference, though, truth be told,

there were hints of a turn of weather. Remember?

All that bluster you took

for courage? All those copperheads you took for care.

CANNIBAL

People are not my thing.

—Cesare Pavese

—they chew and chew and chew and
pinch, pinching off little bits to stuff into
their little mouths, or their wide ones, no
matter, it is the tears that hurt. It takes a lot
of pinching to fill any maw. The
biting down. I have been bitten, chewed
to bits, yet here I am as if without scars. People

don't really see me. Not much to see I suppose
and when they do they usually see vegetable matter
or animal, but seldom a fellow person. No, I am
roughage one eats but doesn't taste, just chew
and swallow down, a quick push past the gullet.

Of course I feel sorry for myself. I am a bit of squash,
the cheese molded on one side, overly soft brined pickle,
all mash and mush. Who wants to be
eaten this way? I expected something different

but knew by adulthood to be honest that this would be
my life: as one taken by others as anything but herself.
Honestly, people leave a bad taste in my mouth.
I don't let them in. Lately, I seem never
to be hungry at all. I am disappearing into the mouth
of heaven perhaps, or hell. Tomato. Tom(ah)to.

The cardinal's plumes are not quite as brightly lit
and the robin brings spring in slowly, as much mud
as grass. The earthworms thrive so the birds are fed
but they take little pleasure from it. A nightingale
trills to all the same song, so none who hear it feel
particularly special. The bluebird is still majestic
but no one notices her through the fog. But the crow,
the same one who forced all the other birds
from the tree, caws out into the gray, perfectly
at home on the blossoming limbs, blossoming
less than the year before. The birds feel it first,
the not quite there. The almost. The this would
be so perfect . . . if . . . if what? they pretend not to know
because to do otherwise would reveal how
frightening paradise is, all of that joy spilling forth.
All of that bliss whose cost, yes, was a bruise or two
or a life of bruising but . . . isn't it worth it? To have
lips soft on the nape whenever lips are needed.
To have a hand pressed into the small of a back
whenever one feels faint after crying it all out at last.

GOAT

for *Idoia*

Capricorn, hair, bray and hoof, eater of tin, biter,
bitter sister, tamer than wild, not quite
gamey as deer, lower cousin to the caribou,
giving rise to tears and the satyr. O Tragos,
in the night I had a memory of sweetgrass
and clover, a nudge of the brow, a lapping tongue—
it swept over me like a breeze through the rails,
leaving when my eyes opened. Child
that I am of Saturn and revels, each moment lives
for each moment until a recollection comes
in a dream that only wounds upon waking,
when the truth of loss is an emptied horn of plenty.
I know you understand having lost and having gained.

FANTASTICA MELANCHOLIA

I have feathers like a bird-of-paradise   I spread them out into a great black fan
and the sun that had droughted everything has no power to the umbrella

of my feathers   glossy   high   as a rainforest's canopy and in such a paradise
no one has a fear of darkness   no one has

a fear of me   under my wings they take swigs of water like   fruited wine
                                          they celebrate the cool and sudden night

When night actually does come I pull my feathers back
I become but a human with two dark arms again

and in them those I love   safe in this embrace?
without fear or repulsion   without

any expectations   but I know
this for the daydream it is   I have no feathers

and like my mother my friends wince in the darkness   the metaphor
for naught   for no   for not now   for never

so I have learned to keep my arms to myself   to arm myself
with sorrow and dreams   my skin lit   by neglect and moonlight

THE DEAD HORSE

Knows its true name
but won't tell you. The dead horse
counts and despises the flies on its
muzzle and remembers the smell
of the shooter. The dead horse
comforts itself by playing dead
and praying the shooter won't return.
The dead horse can tell time and
her dying was slow, month after month.
You could say the dead horse is armored
now, so full of bullets and phlegm.
Didn't you say *Whoa*?
the dead horse held on while its tongue was
removed. Some men like a token.

                              Quiet
now, the dead horse is still not at peace,
though the shooter comes recalling
not that first shot but the last round.
And isn't it good to get it all out? To
leave it in the hide that bucked.

THE CANNIBAL MYTH

If they take you, they will eat you.

       No.
If they take you, they will keep you

and you will eat
              your own hands.

OTA BENGA'S CAGE

St. Louis World's Fair, 1904

He was pampered
the way exotic fish are fed—a few silvery flakes at a time.

We held out bracelets, tin garlands,
buffalo nickels—anything
that glinted, caught in the sun
for a moment, a shimmer to follow across the Atlantic,
aluminum mirrors for his own reflection—quicksilver
smile—twenty-two pointed teeth
that chewed the food we gave him
                                —delicacies:
boiled eggs in pickle brine,
caviar on toasted points,
goose tartare, and palmettos,
all pushed through the bars
whenever he liked! He complained anyway.
We gave him more blankets, chided, petted,
said, *It's not so bad, is it?* We put up with his
whistles, his snorts and odd scratching,
his short chin held up to gauge our reactions.
Amused or angry, he smiled in our faces—
his teeth drawing blood from his own bottom lip.
SEE THE PYGMY, we cried, and pulled
children over, caught the sleeves of their mothers,
gave cigars to the men who couldn't stop staring
at the child? animal? They stooped to look
him straight in his eyes tearing red
as Geronimo's—two cages down.

DARK HORSE

This is not the first time I've spoken of her.
Just a mare. Brown as any mare. My memory
has been tainted by my own age, so I remember
her as an older horse. Given to me because
her time as a hauler was done and her temperament
was gentle, or she had been broken. I don't know which,
maybe both. I loved her as much as a child could. Now,
I love her as much as a woman can, which means
we are indivisible. There is only one picture I have of her
and it is not on paper but in the mind: I am upon her
with my thin arms around her neck. No saddle, so
I could feel her as part of myself through the blanket.
It is easy to see she would move slowly as I do now.
I can feel the throb of her blood moving through
our dark body. And I know it for love. Not the only love
I would have. But the truest. What did the mare feel
of me? I would say, everything.

ACKNOWLEDGMENTS

Some of the poems in this book have appeared in various versions in the following journals and anthologies:

A Face to Meet the Faces: An Anthology of Contemporary Persona Poetry, "The Wheel of the Bus: A Fiction"

African American Review, "The Keening"

Afrique Noir, "The Winter Kingdom"

Another and Another: A Grind Anthology, "*The World Contracts*"

Asheville Review, "I Am the Only One I Know Who Can Cook Them, and My Grandpa Did, Was in Fact Known for Several Counties Round for His Way with a Pot, So"

Asheville Review, *Best American Poetry* 2019, "Canzone in Blue, Then Bluer"

Barrow Street, "I've Worn It Three Days in a Row"

Blood Root, "The Dead Horse"

Blue Shift Journal, "Everywhere and Here Too"

Callaloo, "Emmett, I Said Wait"

The Common, "*Moan Soft Like You Wanted Someone Terrible*"

The Common, "This Morning I Miss Such Devotion"

Fishouse, "The Wheel of the Bus: A Fiction"

Harvard Review, "Honey"

Harvard Review, "When Your Brother Dies You Want"

Kenyon Review, "Juneteenth (#3)"

Kenyon Review, *Best American Poetry 2022*, "1965"

Sewanee Review, "I've Been Thinking about Love Again"

Sewanee Review, "Uncle Sonny"

spin.com (Spin Magazine), "Marvin Gaye: Mercy"

spin.com (Spin Magazine), "Marvin Gaye: Sugar"

Third Wednesday, "Finding Myself in the Market of Accra"

VQR, "Goat"

VQR, "On the Piney Woods, Death, Bobby Frank Cherry, and Me"

VQR, Best American Poetry 2020, "The Shore"

Waxwing, "A Call to Arms"

Waxwing, "The Shared World"

Yale Review, "Returns"

I would like to thank the following people who have inspired, supported, challenged, motivated, or helped me in their respective ways to see this particular collection of poems through to completion: Curtis Bauer, Alexander Chee, Robert Fanning, Laura Jean Gilloux, Jennifer Grotz, Dr. Ray Howard, Perry Janes, Lannan Foundation at Marfa (that gave me a place to grieve), Joel Lazar and DHC, Trish Marshall, Airea Dee Matthews, Sebastian Matthews, Andrew McCann, Leslie Shipman, the Ricky Gordon Group (love all of you so much), the Roundtop Poetry Festival (who let me free the bones), Still North Books & Bar (thank you, Allie), the Tuckerbox Cafe (especially Michelle), the Tuckerboxers: Sally Ball, Bill Craig, John Greismer, and Peter Orner, my editors Maia Rigas and the astonishing Parneshia Jones (whose generosity is boundless), my family and poet Matthew Scott Olzmann, whose care is where I begin. For those whose names do not appear here, please forgive my oversight and know you are appreciated.